BABY BROTHER JESUS

JOHN ARMSTRONG

Abingdon Press

BABY BROTHER JESUS

Copyright © 1990 by Baby Brother Music

ISBN 0-687-02342-4 Baby Brother Jesus
ISBN 0-687-02343-2 Baby Brother Jesus with Listening Tape
ISBN 0-687-02344-0 Baby Brother Jesus Production Tape

MANUFACTURED IN THE UNITED STATES OF AMERICA

"Jesus is not ashamed to call us his brothers" (Hebrews 2:11 TLB).

At Christmas God himself came to become one of us. In the baby we see our heritage and our hope. He is the Holy One yet we share the same Father. When Jesus was born the world had a new baby brother, Baby Brother Jesus.

We first performed *Baby Brother Jesus* to an enthusiastic crowd at St. Paul's United Methodist Church in Mt. Juliet, Tennessee in December 1987. In the following years till its publication, it evolved into its present form due to a lot of prayer, hard work, and helpful suggestions from the members of the casts and audience. I acknowledge and appreciate their contributions. I hope the people of St. Paul's will always see themselves in my music.

When you perform *Baby Brother Jesus* please follow their example and mold the performance to speak to your congregation or audience. The personal touches you add to the music, costumes, or staging will allow God to speak to the people you know.

Baby Brother Jesus is intended to show that God came to our world to become our brother. Hopefully the mood and the music will help your people remember that Christmas is really about love, not fighting crowds and spending money.

John Armstrong

DIRECTOR'S INSTRUCTIONS

The main purpose of the chancel drama, Baby Brother Jesus, is to express the significance of the birth of Jesus Christ to as many people as possible.

As wonderful as the birth was, everything around at that time was simple: the surroundings, stable, stalls, animals; Mary and Joseph all alone, no Neo-Natal surgeon on standby should there be any complications; it was just a simple birth with shepherds and wise men. Simple . . . and this is the focus for the staging of Baby Brother Jesus.

Keeping in mind that the music and lyrics are the main focus, the stage can be and should be simple. Most churches perform right in the chancel, thus, "chancel drama."

Lighting

A few spot lights can be used to highlight the singers, and they can either come forward to a specific microphone, or may sing where they are in the pulpit with a follow spot moving to their location.

Instruments

Originally *Baby Brother Jesus* was performed simply with a guitar. This concept lends to the tenderness of the music and thoughts and can be reserved for special moments like Mary's song and perhaps the shepherds and wise men quartets. If anyone would like to accompany themselves on the guitar or keyboard, that would be fine, just keep in mind the location of the piano so the people can see the singer. The entire performance can be done with a guitar, keyboard, or combination of both: A complete performance tape is available through Baby Brother Music Productions should you choose to use a tape system. Check your local bookstore for ordering.

Narration

The narrator can be anywhere you would like. Several suggestions are: sitting in an armchair off to the side with a floor-light to turn on and off when speaking, moving about the stage and using a follow-spot, standing where the minister delivers the sermons, or sitting among the singers on stage and standing up on the narration. Whatever works well for your setting will be just fine.

Vocals

Most of the music is written for average-ranged solo singing with a couple of exceptions. There are times when the age of a specific performer might enhance the part; however, these are not definites. They are only suggestions, and any and all age groups can perform this work. (Refer to the individual parts for specifics on the vocals.)

The cast may be made up of only the number required, or your full choir may be on stage. The group numbers are usually in addition to a solo—for example, "Blessed Is He," which is also known as the "prophet song," is sung by the soloist with all the cast members singing on the choruses, and the same happens on the ending title song, "Baby Brother Jesus."

"Christmas Song": The verses of this opening song should be sung either by one or two people. If for example a man and woman sing it, the first verse is sung by the man, the second by the woman and the third, jointly in tertial harmony. The chorus can be sung by all the cast members, in harmony.

"Blessed Is He": All verses are to be sung by a lower voice. The chorus is to be sung by all the cast members, in harmony.

"Under the Law": A male duet. If one could play the harmonica, that would be great to enhance the vocal lines, such as on the third and fourth beats of the measures. Have fun with this song; the message is serious, but it is comedy in its performance.

"The Way of the Lord": Elizabeth's song. May be sung by an older woman so as to enforce the dramatics of what God did for her and her husband.

"Joseph's Song": A second tenor voice may be used. Age doesn't really matter. A younger person may assist with the visuals and help bring home the impact God has on this young man's life. Director's option.

"Mary's Song": Someone is needed with a mezzo woman's range and control on long-sustaining lyric lines. Again, age really doesn't matter. However, consideration should be given to the age of the person playing Joseph to ensure continuity.

"Who Is This?": A children's song. The children are imitating the animals in the stall. Your children's choir or children in the cast may sing this. Make sure the microphones are such that the children can sing together.

"A New Day": A rock and roll angel song. Chorus sings background glorias. A spotlight should be on the soloist.

"Shepherds and Wise Men": A comedy song to be sung by two sets of quartets with a mixture of male and female voices. The shepherds sing in unison with a strong "country" sound and the wise men sing in strict but flowing four-part harmony. The last verse and chorus are sung by both the shepherds and wise men and are sung in four part harmony with the shepherds maintaining their country flavor. The two groups can move together for verse three to show the unity of God's people.

"Baby Brother Jesus": The same person or people used in the opening song may be used for the verses. However, different people may be used, depending on the capability of the cast members. The entire cast stands and sings on the chorus.

Costumes

Baby Brother Jesus is intended to be contemporary and simple. It is suggested that the performers wear normal, casual clothing with these exceptions:

"Under the Law": A suggestion for the blues singer(s) would be black suit, white shirt, black hat and tie, and sunglasses.

"Who is This?": The children can wear jogging suits or sweat shirts of subdued colors. We have used bells hung on ribbons worn around the neck to suggest that they are farm animals.

"Shepherds and Wise Men": The shepherds can be dressed as cowboys while the wisemen should be dressed as professors, bankers, or other professionals. Graduation cap and gown, clerical collar, or other symbols of wisdom could be born by one or more of the wisemen. We have always included men and women in both quartets.

Angel: We have always used traditional angel attire (white robe and halo).

Remember that *Baby Brother Jesus* should be tailored to suit your audience or congregation. Let your costumes—whether contemporary or traditional, simple or elaborate—be chosen to best present the characters' stories to your people.

Staging

The blues singers, angel, and children are normally offstage until their entrance, and then join the choir after their songs. All other characters take the stage at the beginning of the performance as the choir, with soloists moving up to microphones.

Rehearsals

You may find it easier to schedule rehearsals for the soloists and quartets first and then have two or three dress rehearsals for the whole cast nearer to the performance date. This is helpful since the roles are essentially independent of each other and are no trouble to put together once the individuals or groups know their parts. It is especially easy for the children not to have to sit through long rehearsals.

"We who have been made holy by Jesus, now have the same Father he has. That is why Jesus is not ashamed to call us his brothers. For he says in the book of Psalms, 'I will talk to my brothers about God my Father, and together we will sing his praises.' At another time he said, 'I will put my trust in God along with my brothers.' And at still another time, 'See, here am I and the children God gave me.' Since we, God's children, are human beings—made of flesh and blood—he became flesh and blood too by being born in human form; for only as a human being could he die and in dying break the power of the devil who had the power of death. Only in that way could he deliver those who through fear of death have been living all their lives as slaves to constant dread. We all know he did not come as an angel but as a human being—yes, a Jew. And it was necessary for Jesus to be like us, his brothers, so that he could be our merciful and faithful High Priest before God, a Priest who would be both merciful to us and faithful to God in dealing with the sins of the people. For since he himself has now been through suffering and temptation, he knows what it is like when we suffer and are tempted, and he is wonderfully able to help us" (Hebrews 2:11-18 TLB).

CHRISTMAS SONG

John Armstrong

night of Je- sus' com- ing, known to just a few. And most of them are won- der- ing ex- act- ly what to do. For to some Christ is a Di- e- ty, and to some he is a man, but to- night he is a

9

lit- tle _ child; that's ea- sy to un- der- _ stand.

All the an- i- mals and shep- _ herds _ can on- ly just look _

on. But Ma- ry _ thinks _ a _- bout these things when ev- ery- one is

gone. For to some he is a con- quer- _ or and to

some the Prince of _ Peace. But to her he is _ a _ ba- by, who

must be _ rocked to _ sleep.

It's o- kay if we _ don't _

un- der- _ stand ev- ery- thing that God has _ done. If we

come. For to some he is _ a tea- cher, and to

some the King _ of _ kings, but to- night he is _ a _

lit- tle child, who made the an- gels sing. For to

D.S. al coda

D.S. al coda

12

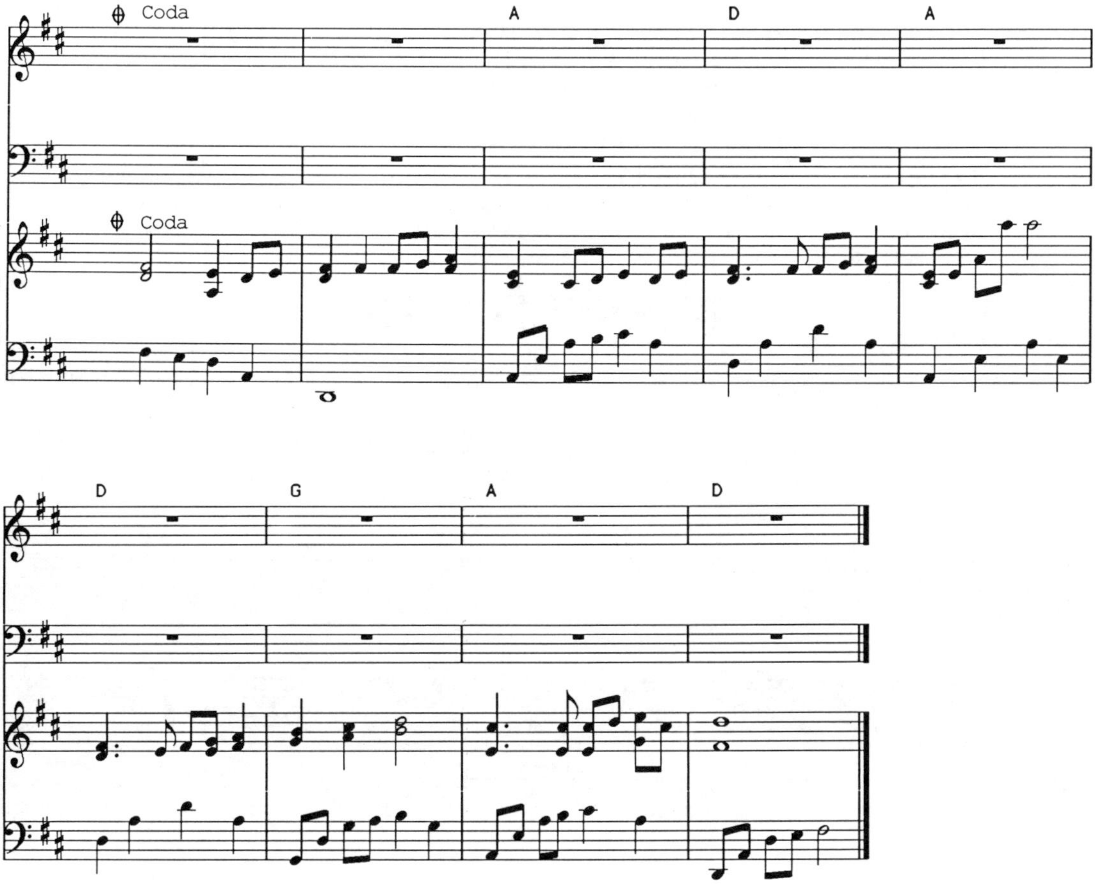
Coda
A
D
A
Coda
D
G
A
D

Silent Night. Holy Night. When we think of Christmas, we tend to think of one night, don't we? One special night. But that night is really only one part of the never ending story of how God chooses to work in the world. And he almost always chooses to work through people. People like you. People like me. People like the Israelites.

The Israelites had looked for their Messiah for centuries. Their prophets had talked about his coming for over a thousand years. The prophet Isaiah said "for to us a child is born, to us a son is given; and the government will be upon his shoulder, and his name will be called 'Wonderful Counselor, Mighty God, Everlasting Father, Prince of Peace' " (Isaiah 9:6).

BLESSED IS HE

John Armstrong

talks a-bout peace and sal- va- tion, and says our God is King.

shout with joy to- geth- er, as he re- turns to our place.

Bles- sed is he who comes in the name of the Lord,
(melody)

of the Lord. Bles- sed is he who

comes in the name of the Lord, of the Lord.

Like a sap-ling, he grew up be-fore _us, like a green tree in the des-ert land. Sure-ly he has born our suf- ferings, and by his wounds we are healed.

Bles- sed is he who comes in the name __ of the Lord,

of the Lord, __ Bles- sed is he who

comes in the name __ of the Lord, __ of the Lord.

Did you ever wonder why the Israelites looked for a messiah? Well, they were convinced that they were God's chosen people. The Messiah would deliver them from their problems. And what problems these chosen people had. They had been slaves in Egypt, and captives in Babylon. They had fought with every nation that was anywhere near them.

And then there was the law. You see, the Israelites had one path to salvation, one way to God. And that was the law—God's law. If they kept all the rules, if they obeyed the law, then they were right with God. But they couldn't do it. They were frustrated by a standard that was impossible to meet.

The book of Amos speaks of "professional lamenters"; people who mourned the situation Israel was in. I guess you could say they were the blues singers of their day. But then, when you're under the law like they were, what can you do but sing the blues?

UNDER THE LAW

John Armstrong

rock'in
I woke up this morn- ing, I was un- der the law.

When I went to work, I was un- der the law. I stay up all night try ing to for-

get a- bout it all. I feel it come- ing down __ on me. I know

_ when times are hard, you've got to be tough. But when it comes to this law, _ you know I just ain't good e- nough. _ In my heart I know _ there ought to be a bet- ter way, _ I hope that I can find it some- day.

When I do right, I'm un- der the law. When I do wrong,

I'm un- der the law.   I stay up all night trying to for- get a- bout it all,   I

feel it com- ing down _ on   me.   I know

2. G7

C7   G7   C7

G7   C7   G7

21

Ev'ry- thing that I own, is un- der the law.

My wife and my fam- ily, they're un- der the law. My dog and my cat,

they're un- der the law. I feel it com- ing down __ on me.

I know __ when times are hard, you've

got to be tough. But when it comes to this law _ you know I

just ain't good e- nough. _ In my heart I know _ there ought to

be a bet- ter way, _ I hope that I can find it some- day. I know

day

"In the days of Herod, king of Judea, there was a priest named Zechariah, of the division of Abijah; and he had a wife of the daughters of Aaron, and her name was Elizabeth. And they were both righteous before God, walking in all the commandments and ordinances of the Lord blameless. But they had no child, because Elizabeth was barren, and both were advanced in years" (Luke 1:5-7).

There are a lot of people mentioned in the Bible who were a part of the story of Jesus. Most of them were very ordinary people just living out their lives day by day. Then Jesus happened and they became a part of something special and important. Just look at Elizabeth. She was years older than her cousin Mary. Her husband was a priest in the synagogue. They had wanted a child but had never been able to have one. And now Elizabeth was past the age when most women could have children. How could she have known? Throughout all the years that Elizabeth had prayed for a child, how could she have guessed that in God's time she would become the mother of the one who would announce the Messiah's arrival, the one called John the Baptist. If only she had known God's plan, how different her life would have been. But isn't that just like God—to take someone who thinks she's just living out her days and show her she's part of his plan. It was the way of the Lord that she should stop being the "barren one," and become the blessed one (Luke 1:36).

THE WAY OF THE LORD

John   Armstrong

E♭ B♭ Gmi B♭/C Cmi
see him now. I've want- ed all my life
ones like me. Who think they've missed their chance
F E♭ B♭
to have this child some- how. To think he'd
to meet with des- ti- ny. The years that
A♭/E♭ E♭ Cmi7 F E♭ B♭
be the _ one to an- nounce the Ho- ly Son.
dragged on _ by, they seem like mo- ments now.
Gmi B♭/E♭ E♭6 F
It is the way of the Lord, for this to
It is the way of the Lord, for this to

E♭/B♭ B♭ Cmi Dmi F/E♭ E♭
be. If I had on- ly known
be. If I had on- ly known
F E♭/B♭ B♭ Gmi
that it would be this way, my life would
that it would be this way, I would have
B♭/E♭ E♭ F E♭ B♭ Cmi Dmi
have been changed from _ that ve- ry day. If some- how
thought much less of my sad yes- ter- days. The pain that
F/E♭ E♭ F E♭ B♭
I had seen, how close we'd be to- day.
went be- fore would not have held me down.

Gmi
B♭/E♭
E♭6
F
That I would fi- nally know the way of the
If I had on- ly seen the way of the
E♭/B♭
1.B♭
2.B♭
Cmi
B♭/D
D.S. al coda
Lord.
Lord.
It is the
If I had
1.
2.
D.S. al coda
B♭
Coda
B♭/E♭
E♭6
F
G♭
That I would fi- nally know the way of the Lord.
Coda
E♭mi7
B♭

"Now the birth of Jesus Christ took place in this way. When his mother Mary had been betrothed to Joseph, before they came together, she was found to be with child of the Holy Spirit; and her husband Joseph, being a just man and unwilling to put her to shame, resolved to divorce her quietly. But as he considered this, behold, an angel of the Lord appeared to him in a dream saying, 'Joseph, son of David, do not fear to take Mary your wife, for that which is conceived in her is of the Holy Spirit; she will bear a son, and you shall call his name Jesus, for he will save his people from their sins' " (Matthew 1:18-21).

Yes, Elizabeth had waited a long time to know the way of the Lord. But what about Joseph? How was he introduced to God's plan? Well, just as he prepared to begin married life, Joseph found out that his new bride, the girl of his dreams, was pregnant! This wasn't just bad news. It was dangerous news. Mary could be stoned for adultery. The scripture states that Joseph "wished to put her away secretly." This could have been for her protection, or to hide his shame. But he didn't turn against her and justify it with the law. Instead, Joseph listened to what God had to say.

JOSEPH'S SONG

John Armstrong

In our lit- _ tle town _ one night, _ ev- ry- thing was go- _ ing just _ right, when I asked her if _ she'd be _ my _ wife. But now strange things _ are hap- pen- ing, and I don't know what _ to do. _ But I think it's going

to change _ _ my life. Cause

some- one told _ me in a dream,
cause He

things aren't al- _ ways

what they _ seem, _ don't _ give up on _ the one _ you know is true. Now some may say __ that I __ am wrong,

but I've loved __ her for __ so __ long. __ I'm gon- na do the things

__ she needs __ me __ to. Some in town __ will frown

__ and say __ that I should turn __ __ a- way, __

31

be-cause of the things __ they say __ she's __ done.

But I think God ____ spoke to me,

and in my heart __ I be- lieve, __ this child will be

__ the pro- __ __ mised one. Cause

Some- _ times it's hard to try _ to fol- low God and not _ know why _

He does things the way _ he seems _ to _ do.

But I know it's through _ his car- _ ing,

and the love _ we're shar- _ ing, the world _ will come

to know _ _ him too. Be-

D.S. al coda

D.S. al coda

34

"In those days a decree went out from Caesar Augustus that all the world should be enrolled. This was the first enrollment, when Quirinius was governor of Syria. And all went to be enrolled, each to his own city. And Joseph also went up from Galilee, from the City of Nazareth, to Judea, to the city of David, which is called Bethlehem, because he was of the house and lineage of David, to be enrolled with Mary, his betrothed, who was with child" (Luke 2:1-5).

Life wasn't easy for Mary. She knew what the people were probably saying. And even with a strong faith in God's plan, she must have wondered why—why does it have to be this way? Why must her son, the Messiah, be born during the time of the census? Why isn't the birth of the king important to everyone? And why, after traveling so far, must they stay in a cold, dirty stable, neglected and alone?

ROAD TO BETHLEHEM

John Armstrong

for me to tra- vel on. ___ If it was- n't

bad e- nough ___ to bear the shame ___

of a child ___ who al- most

had no name. ___ now they're rid- ing me a- to-
sleep out- side a- now I know it's

36

Emi G D/F# Emi
round on rough and rock- y ground; I don't
night, I just don't think it's right; but I don't
time, but in- side my mind, I don't
A7sus A Asus A Asus A Asus
know why it has to be
know
know
A
this way. It's a
1. D
small town,
Ami7
this Beth- le hem. It's a

small town, ___ with _ so ma-ny here.

Now I can see _____ _____ there's no

place to stay; _____ _____ I have to say _____

_____ I've seen bet-ter days. _____ _____ and if I

cold town, _____ _____ _ this Beth- le- _ hem, no- bo- dy cares _____ _____ all that much. It's not all that bad, _____ the way they've treat- ed me. _ _ _ But is

Bmi7 · · · · Esus

this the way —— —— they'll treat him, — too?

E · · D.S. al coda · Coda Asus A Asus A Asus A

And why it has — to be — this way. ——

D.S. al coda · Coda

A

40

"And while they were there, the time came for her to be delivered. And she gave birth to her first-born son and wrapped him in swaddling cloths, and laid him in a manger, because there was no place for them in the inn" (Luke 2:6-7).

What an honor it would have been to have the Messiah born in your house. Most people would expect this honor to come to the wealthiest or most powerful person in town. Or to the family with the biggest, most luxurious house.

So who did God choose? Who was honored by having the Christ child as a guest? The animals! Lowly sheep, calves, and lambs who couldn't possibly understand who their guest was.

WHO IS THIS

John Armstrong

Lyrics under the staff:
Who is this in-side our house? We real-ly want to
Je- sus who's in-side our house; we'll keep him safe and

Lyrics (line 1):
know. We would have liked to fix things up and
spread the hay just so. He didn't make us clean our stalls, He
just came right on in. We know our house is
good e-nough; it's good e-nough for him. He is the one who

Lyrics (line 2):
dry. We'll be still and let him sleep, and
we won't make him cry. His moth-er sings so soft to him; we
like to lis-ten too. He can stay in-
side our house. as long as He wants to.

Verse (lyrics):

let us know, that we are spe- cial too. He can stay in-

side our house as long as he wants to. It's long as He wants

to.

"And in that region there were shepherds out in the field, keeping watch over their flock by night. And an angel of the Lord appeared to them, and the glory of the Lord shone around them, and they were filled with fear. And the angel said to them, 'Be not afraid; for behold, I bring you good news of a great joy which will come to all the people; for to you is born this day in the city of David a Savior, who is Christ the Lord. And this will be a sign for you: you will find a babe wrapped in swaddling cloths and laying in a manger.' And suddenly there was with the angel a multitude of the heavenly host praising God and saying, 'Glory to God in the highest, and on earth peace among men with whom he is pleased!' " (Luke 2:8-14).

I wonder what kind of music the angels sang on that most holy of nights. Many people think it was probably some kind of sacred church music. And maybe it was. Maybe it was a heavenly music that we can't even imagine. But it might have been whatever type of music the shepherds could understand. Maybe certain songs were picked just for the shepherds, to bring them to their feet and move them to the manger. Maybe if it happened today it could even be rock 'n' roll.

A NEW DAY STARTS TONIGHT

John Armstrong

there is a sta- _ ble and a bed __ of hay.

There's a ba- by cry- _ ing, but its a hap- py _ day.

He's come to live and die, __ __

to take our blues a- way. __

Its time for peace on earth;

Bb ... F

(choir) Glo- ri- a / its time for good- will. Glo- ri- a

C ... Bb7

Now you know what you're worth. Glo- ri- a / why are You stand-ing still?

F ... Bb

Go see what's come to pass; Glo- ri- a

F

the dark has changed to light. Glo- ri- a / The slaves are free at last;

46

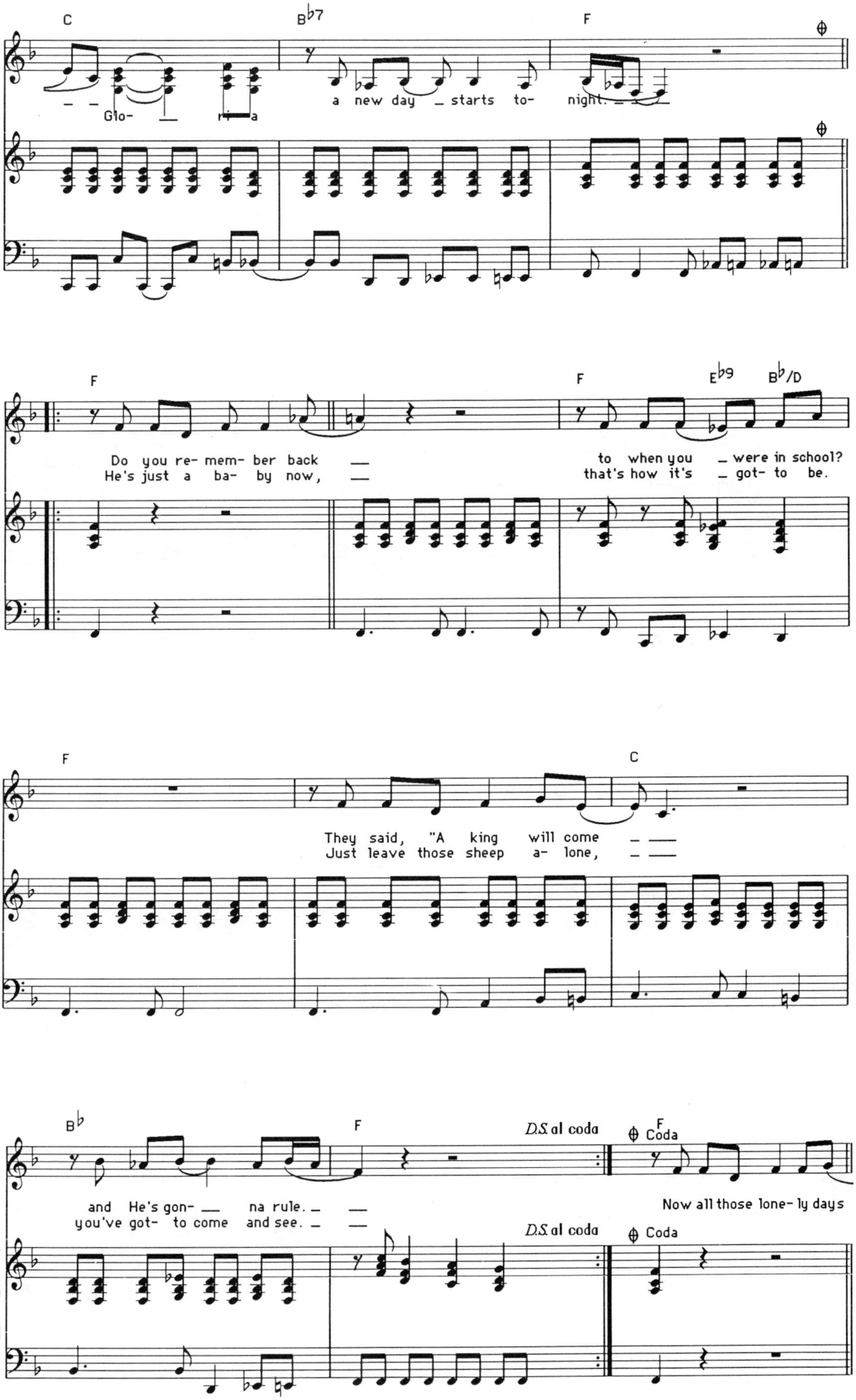

Lyrics (vocal line):

Glo- — ri- a a new day _ starts to- night. _

Do you re-mem-ber back _ to when you _ were in school?
He's just a ba- by now, _ that's how it's _ got- to be.

They said, "A king will come - —
Just leave those sheep a- lone, - —

and He's gon- — na rule. _ —
you've got- to come and see. _ —

D.S. al coda ⊕ Coda

Now all those lone- ly days

are just a mem- o- ry, —

and this is just a taste — of your e- ter- ni- ty. —

I think we both know why,

al- though I don't know how — But I know God him- self

is sleep- ing in a man- ger now. Its time for peace on earth,

Glo- ri- a it's time _ _ for good- will, _ _ Glo- ri- a

now you know what you're worth, _ Glo- ri- a why are you stand- ing still. _

_ _ _ Go see what's come to pass; Glo- ri- a

the dark has changed to light. Glo- ri- a The slaves are free at last;

-- Glo- ri- a a new day _ starts to- night. _ _

Slaves are free at last, _ _ a new day _ starts to-

night. _ _

"When the angels went away from them into heaven, the shepherds said to one another, 'Let us go over to Bethlehem and see this thing that has happened, which the Lord has made known to us.' And they went with haste, and found Mary and Joseph, and the babe lying in a manger. And when they saw it they made known the saying which had been told them concerning this child; and all who heard it wondered at what the shepherds told them" (Luke 2:15-18).

"Now when Jesus was born in Bethlehem of Judea in the days of Herod the king, behold, wise men from the East came to Jerusalem, saying, 'Where is he who has been born king of the Jews? For we have seen his star in the East, and have come to worship him.' . . . When they had heard the king they went their way; and lo, the star which they had seen in the East went before them, till it came to rest over the place where the child was. When they saw the star, they rejoiced exceedingly with great joy" (Matthew 2:1-2, 9-10).

Shepherds and wise men. Two groups invited to see the baby. The shepherds were probably the least educated, lowest paid, most common people in town. After all, watching sheep is not a career goal many of us would choose for ourselves.

The wise men were just the opposite. They were a well educated, finely dressed group. And considering the gifts they brought, they were obviously rich, too.

So what did these two groups have in common? They both took the time to listen. To let God tell them about the baby. The wise men were quietly searching the books, the traditions, and the stars. The shepherds were just quiet. Both groups found the baby, and all of their lives were changed.

SHEPHERDS AND WISEMEN

John Armstrong

Some- times it's hard to find Je- sus, —

ev- en if you're told the way to go. Seems like this town is full of

sta- bles, __ which one is the one, we just don't know. As

shep- herds you know we're not no- ted __ for be- ing the smart- est folks around. But still we're proud to be cho- sen, ___ and

we won't stop un- til that boy is found.

Some- times it's hard to find Je- sus, es-
Now we're so glad we found Je- sus.

pecial- ly if you've come a long, long way. We've
It was worth _ all the work and pain. We

fol- lowed his star _ for so long now,
don't know ex- act- ly for what we're do- ing,

seems like we should be there a-ny- day. As wise- men you know that we're
but we know we'll nev- er be the same. And now _ you know that we're

no- ted for be- ing the smart- est folks a- round. — — —
no- ted, for be- in' the happi- est folks a- round. — — —

But it hum- bles us to be cho- sen, — and
And _ we're so glad we were cho- sen, —

Bb7   1. Eb   2. Eb

we won't stop un- til that boy is   found.   found.
and that He let Him- self be

Bb   Eb

We did- n't stop un- til that boy was   found!
found, that boy was found!

The differences between the shepherds and the wise men remind us that Jesus came to earth for everyone, not just a certain few. People like you and me, with all of our problems and unfulfilled dreams, can become essential parts of God's greatest miracle.

Remember Elizabeth, counting the years with no child. Remember Mary and Joseph, enduring the ridicule and criticism of their friends and neighbors because they believed the child was the new king of Israel. How did they feel when he was born in a stable among the animals? Think of the shepherds, living their quiet, unimpressive lives until Jesus made them special. Remember the wise men and their journey, foretold years before, and the excitement they must have felt.

A lot of us can identify with the people in this story. But we have problems a little more modern to deal with. Problems like working extra hours at Christmas. Like finding, paying for, and wrapping hundreds of presents. And this time of year reminds us that our families are scattered or broken or that someone is not here this year who was here last year. But at Christmas we need to remember how God takes peoples' sorrows and makes them triumphs for the world. We need to be reminded that God himself came to share all of these things with us, to be one of us. He came to our world to share the good things and to finally conquer the bad things. On that night long ago, he became part of our family, and the world had a new baby brother, Baby Brother Jesus.

BABY BROTHER JESUS

John Armstrong

Well, we've got a ba——by boy to-night, he's

come to bring the peo- _ ple light. _ _ Born to be a sa- cri- fice,

ba- by bro- ther _ Je- sus. _ _ Is- 'nt he a sight to see? He's

ev- ery- thing we thought _ he'd be. _ _ He looks a- lot like you and me, _

ba- by bro- ther _ Je- _ sus.

1. F C G Ami
If you've got no mon- ey, he was born poor too. If your
F C B♭ F/A G
par- ents they were work- ing folks, then he's a lot like you.
F C Ami D7 G
If you feel dis- cour- aged, he's felt that way too. If you
C B♭ F/A
think a- bout how you're like him, there's no tel- ling what you could do.

Be-cause we've He's got rich-es in his home,

there's plen-ty left for you. His Fa-ther is the on-ly one, and

I know he loves you. He had to come down here to show you the

things he knows are true. Where he comes from, the

weak and low- _ ly, have great _ things to do. _

That's why we've ba- by _ bro- ther _

Je- _ sus.

61